385 Kochanek, Ed
KOC   Along an open track

DATE DUE

16 Feb '84	AN 2 9 97		
18 Apr '85	JUN 3 0 97		
OCT 2 3 '85			
NOV 1 8 '85			
DEC 2 7 '85			
FEB 2 1 '86			
MAR 1 5 '86			
MAR 2 2 '88			
MAR 1 9 9			
MAY 02 90			
DEC 1 8 '91			
APR 2 0 '92			
MAY 1 0 '94			
MAR 2 6 '96			
DEC 1 2 96			
JAN 0 8 '97			
GAYLORD			PRINTED IN U.S.A.

S P & S at Marshall, Washington   *Phillip R. Hastings*

Along an Open Track

By

Ed & Sally Kochanek

ACKNOWLEDGMENTS

Without the intense interest of railroad photographers, books like "Along an Open Track" would not be possible. Our thanks to the following photographers for their outstanding work: Don Ahlbeck, Herb Arey, C.W. Burns, Forest Crosseu, B.F. Cutler, Guy L. Dunscomb, Albert Farrow, Jim Fredrickson, Ross Grenard, L.E. Griffith, Henry R. Griffiths, Phillip R. Hastings, Roy Hilner, D.L. Joslyn, Basil Koob, J.W. Lazier, John Maxwell, Neal Miller, Robert P. Olmsted, Otto Perry, E.S. Peyton, Fred Ragsdale, Robert W. Richardson, Emery Roberts, John Shaw, Jim Shaughnessy, Richard Steinheimer, Fred C. Stoes, Jim Walter, Melvin Swansick, Walt Thrall, Dave Wilkie, Dick Wolf. All uncredited photos are from the collection of the author.

CONTENTS

Northwestern Pacific at Tiburon, Calif.   *Richard Steinheimer*

INTRODUCTION

Bear's Stadium in Denver, the scene of popular, exciting baseball in Western League days, provided an excellent view of the Colorado and Southern yard across the South Platte. Many a pleasant summer evening was spent watching switching operations and a 900 or a big Burlington 6100 back out of the house in preparation for the North Local. A 1945 ride on the Denver Zephyr through a steady Nebraska downpour with a stop at McCook where all attention was given to the raging electrical storm which surrounded us — dropping down to Needles on the Colorado River and stepping off the Eastbound El Capitan into 120 degrees amid Mohave Indians in native dress selling their colorful beads and rugs.

The steady pounding exhaust of a Rio Grande helper through the many tunnels on the very edge of the front range of the Rockies, heard every night if the wind was right. Experiences such as these did much to influence this writer in the area of rail photography. For those who have endeavored to achieve complete satisfaction in this field, neither nature or the elements have stood in their path.

Whether cut off from civilization by a treacherous ground blizzard of a Wyoming winter; facing a scorching, dusty Arizona desert; or setting up for a few night exposures at Alamosa in the still, frigid San Luis Valley at -45 below; the dedicated individual would not pass up the opportunity.

A Rail Fan

The narrow gauge roundhouse of the D&RGW at Alamosa, Colorado was quiet at 6 a.m. in the morning in July of 1967. Only two Mikes were steaming softly in anticipation of a possible call to take a train up Cumbres Pass and into Chama, New Mexico. In the cab of the 497, a shovel stands ready to provide the fireman with a good day's work on the heavy grades west of Antonito. Upon reaching Chama, locomotives which have brought their trains from both Alamosa and Durango wait out the night alongside the now rarely used two-stall engine house. September 1965.

Engine Terminal

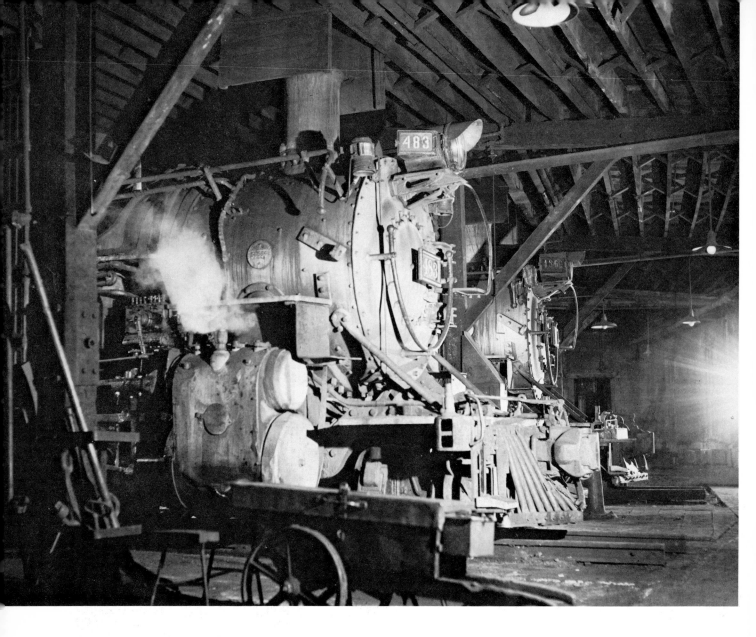

In the Rio Grande roundhouse at Alamosa, once shared by standard gauge steam power, *Jim Shaughnessy* found two of the 480-series 2-8-2's ready for service, above. With the railroad idle during the holidays, the day after Christmas in 1961 brought out the 487 to doublehead with the 494 to Chama, only to be turned back by drifting snow in the vicinity of Sublette.

The dual-gauge yard at Alamosa saw little activity in the summer of 1967, with only an occasional narrow gauge freight and the local freight over La Veta Pass from Walsenburg. Many of the retired narrow gauge 480's and 490's are used for parts in order to keep the remaining engines in operating condition. Below, in a setting complete with the property improvements of "Rio Grande-Land" the 492 is about to leave Durango for Chama in September 1965. On the page opposite, a well maintained Ten-Wheeler of the Nevada Northern emerges from the engine house at East Ely for an excursion assignment in April 1957. *John E. Shaw.*

Some of the Union Pacific 400-series 2-8-0's, built in the early 1900's, were in service almost as long as the Big Boys. They worked on branch lines out of Columbus and Grand Island, Nebraska, where the 490 was photographed in September 1957, opposite. In the spring of 1953, the Colorado & Southern roundhouse in Trinidad, Colorado held 2-10-2 911 and the 372, a high-drivered Pacific which was once Burlington 2965. *Philip R. Hastings.* Before the Monarch Branch was standard gauged and dieselized in the spring of 1956, Mikes of the 480-series such as the 483, standing beside standard gauge. 4-8-4 1801, were assigned to this run west out of Salida, Colorado. September 27, 1952. *Philip R. Hastings.* Below, the Frisco had outdoor engine terminal facilities at Monett, Missouri. *Fred Ragsdale.*

Switching duties and branch line runs completed for the day, the Northern Pacific terminal at Bozeman, Montana holds a line of small motive power, headed by 1389, a trim Ten-Wheeler. July 4, 1951. Opposite, Missouri Pacific 2-8-0 943 is being tied up for the night by the Hostler after handling a local freight over part of the San Antonio, Uvalde & Gulf branch in southern Texas, not far from the border of Mexico. Carrizo Springs, Texas. August 14, 1948. Two photos, *Philip R. Hastings*. August of 1962 found unit 9955 over one of the servicing pits in the Burlington's Denver diesel shops. With the line of the San Luis Valley Southern from Blanca south to Jaroso abandoned, snow-laden steam power is cold and idle in the open-roofed engine house at Blanca. Now operated as the 1.3 mile Southern San Luis Valley R.R., a connection with the Rio Grande is made at Blanca, situated at the southern end of the Sangre de Cristo Range east of Alamosa, Colorado. December 1961.

Often overlooked by the presence of
larger and more prominent Duluth, M
abe & Iron Range, the Duluth & Nor
eastern operates some 11 miles of tr
between Saginaw and Cloquet, Mir
where 2-8-0 16 takes water on Jan. 26, 19
Great Northern's Hillyard engine termi
was also home for SP&S locomotives, s
as the impressive 4-6-6-4's 900 and
below. Two photos, *Philip R. Hastir*
The last steam operation of the Union
cific into Nebraska put several 4-6-6-4's
the 3700-class to work between Sidney a
Cheyenne, Wyo. for a period of almo
three weeks in July 1959. Opposite,
3712 waits in Sidney for servicing and
return trip west, as most of these engi
were kept busy around the clock and p
vided many unforgettable sights dur
these few final days. Surrounded by re
nants of steam days, even these now
thing of the past, Union Pacific turbine
idles under the huge coaling tower
Cheyenne in November 1960.

Even as late as 1957, Union Pacific
Boys filled the roundhouse, were still b
overhauled in the back shop for ano
few months service, and Cheyenne
bustling with activity as the end of st
power was very much in sight. Two pho
Philip R. Hastings. To those who have
served, these Big Boys seemed even n
impressive during the hours of dark
than during the day. Opposite, *J
Shaughnessy* found 4011 about to ease
tremendous weight off the 135 foot t
table at Laramie, Wyoming.

Again featuring the Big Boy, a class of locomotive built only for the Union Pacific, number 4019 stands at the head of a westbound freight in Cheyenne on a very cold August morning in 1958. The 4013, above, was kept especially busy during the latter part of August, 1958. Having brought a westbound in from Cheyenne, the hour is now approaching midnight, the 4013 will soon be called for a return trip—then photographed again early the following morning working hard on still another westbound assignment over Sherman Hill, as seen on page 85.

Main
Lines
West

With 96 cars in tow, Rock Island
4-8-4 5104 passes the depot at
Lawrence, Kansas on its way to
Kansas City. January 7, 1950.
Robert P. Olmsted.

In Chicago's Northwestern Station, the [...] year old City of Denver has arrived aft[er] overnight journey from Denver. August [...] *L. E. Griffith.* For many years the Chica[go &] North Western handled Union Pacific [trains] between Chicago and Omaha. The 1946 ve[rsion] of the San Francisco Overland, now re[duced] to a single coach for passengers and a sch[edule] only from Omaha to Laramie, is westbou[nd at] Cortland, Illinois behind C&NW 4-8-4 [...] The C&NW extends 790 miles west [of] Omaha to Lander, in west-central Wyomi[ng. A] depot is maintained there though the lin[e has] not seen mixed train service for many y[ears.] A hand-operated turntable and the aband[oned] two-stall roundhouse were still on the sce[ne.] September 1964.

Burlington's original Zephyr, later given the name "Pioneer Zephyr", and the Mark Twain Zephyrs operated as the Advance Denver Zephyrs while the 12-car Denver Zephyrs were being built. Above opposite, the 9902 heads west at the Harlem Ave. suburban station just out of Berwyn, Illinois in June 1936. *L. E. Griffith*. Below, the Fast Mail of the Great Northern has left the St. Paul station bound for Minneapolis and the Pacific Northwest behind 4-8-4 2582. Rail Photo Service; *B. F. Cutler*. Here, rolling south near Des Plaines, Ill. is the Duluth-Chicago train of the Soo Line, headed by Pacific 2710. June 1948. *Fred C. Stoes*.

Two views, above and opposite, show the scenic line of the Illinois Central which extends across the state of Iowa and into Omaha, Neb. The Mike on the Boone River bridge at Webster City is handling an eastbound freight in October 1952. The 4-8-2 2401, often used in earlier day passenger service, is working upgrade with heavy tonnage out of Ft. Dodge. Two photos, *Basil W. Koob*. Into Kansas City comes Missouri Pacific train 2/106, the second section of the "Marathon", predecessor of the Missouri River Eagle. Pacifics of the 1100-series were used on this train, but when a second section was required, the 6400's, such as the 6438, were called upon. February 25, 1940. *Dick Wolf*.

Union Pacific 9000's, a unique 4-12-2 type, assigned to the Kansas Division are shown opposite in the vicinity of Lawrence in the eastern part of the state. The 9053 is on an eastbound extra in December 1951 while a September 1949 meet is staged with 9052 on eastbound time freight 472 and Rock Island 4-8-4 5101 westbound with a 70 car extra. Above, 7029 and 5015, a 4-8-2 and 2-10-2 respectively, doublehead number 154 from western Kansas east toward Kansas City. December 16, 1951. Three photos, *Robert P. Olmsted*.

31

...ction at San Antonio, Texas finds the ...orthbound "Texas Special" being a well-...aintained Katy Pacific, opposite, while on ...his page the "Argonaut" arrives on the ...unset Route from New Orleans in August ...948. *Philip R. Hastings.* Dallas Union Sta-...on, served by most of the major south-...estern roads, is the setting for Cotton ...elt 675, once of the Florida East Coast, ...etting under way with the "Lone Star". ...pposite, a big 4-8-2 of the Texas & Pa-...ific hurries out of Dallas in Feb. 1946. ...oth, *Robert W. Richardson.*

Lawrence, Kansas in Dec. 1951 was the scene here of Union Pacific and Rock Island steam power. Train 37, the westbound Pon Express, has taken water before leaving Lawrence in the early hours of the morning behind 4-8-4 817. Below, a 4-12-2, built onl for the Union Pacific, heads west on 1st 357 on a very cold Dec. 14. The Rock Island, with trackage rights over the Union Pa cific between Kansas City and Topeka, sends 4-8-4 5105 west at Midland, Kansas, a siding just out of Lawrence. 3 photo *Robert P. Olmsted.*

Left, Union Pacific 3705, run as a light engine from Denver the night before, stands at the head of a train for Julesburg and points east on a sub-zero January morning in 1954 at Sterling, Colorado. Below, the Union Pacific, caught in a wartime motive power shortage, doubleheaded eastbound tonnage into Cheyenne with locomotives purchased from the Chesapeake & Ohio and Norfolk & Western. *C. W. Burns.*

In July 1959, the last year of steam in regular service on the Union Pacific, several 3700's were kept busy on the main line between Cheyenne and Sidney, Nebraska, where the 3708 is seen heading west on one of the last runs.

Burlington's Pioneer Zephyr, having made history in 1934 on the Chicago-Denver run, found its way to the Colorado & Souther in 1949 and replaced steam powered trains 31 and 32 in daytime round-trip service between Denver and Cheyenne. Two view show it on February 26, 1950 in the Wyoming capital city loading for the return trip. A few years later, in January 1957, Unio Pacific 3822 is in Cheyenne on Denver-bound No. 334, a mixed train with a somewhat slower schedule, arriving in Denver jus before midnight after an early evening departure.

n from the eastbound City of Denver at LaSalle, Colorado is
ion Pacific No. 52, a local from Cheyenne to Denver, behind
cific 2897 which often handled this assignment as it did this day
March 1955. Below, during the last big show of steam operation
the Colorado & Southern in the fall of 1958, the 807 and 900 team
with southbound tonnage a few miles east of Boulder, Colorado
h the Continental Divide providing the background.

Once again Colorado & Southern 807 is called for service on the north local near Berthoud, Colorado in February 1959 while one year later northbound 77 parallels the new diagonal highway between Boulder and Longmont after a freshly fallen snow. Above, the 638, used for many excursions before its retirement in the city of Trinidad, works upgrade near Louisville, Colorado with a special in September 1962.

In the days before train sheds, narrow and standard gauge trains await departure from an earlier Denver Union Depot, the present structure being built in 1924. In 1951, Union Pacific's Pony Express heads west from Denver behind big 4-8-4 No. 830. Rail Photo Service: *B. F. Cutler*. In a view emphasizing its 77″ drivers, Union Pacific 809, one of the last of the class to operate into Denver, stands in the station on the National Parks Special in the summer of 1952. *Richard Steinheimer*.

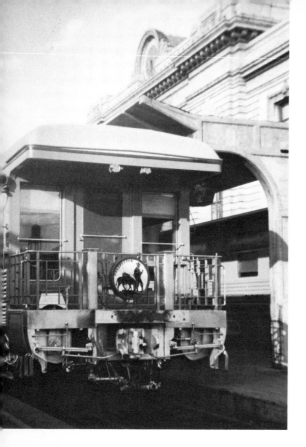

Having operated on the Denver & Rio Grande for over 25 years, originally as a two unit diesel-electric motor car train, the Prospector ended its service in May 1967 and has gone the way of many Rio Grande trains which offered some of the most spectacular scenery of any Western road — The Scenic Limited, Panoramic, Mountaineer, Exposition Flyer, The Royal Gorge. With the future of the California Zephyr and Yampa Valley Mail in doubt, the last passenger service may well be on the narrow gage. Here, in 1952, the Prospector is in Denver Union Terminal while below, after a heavy spring snow, it is descending the eastern slope of the Rockies below Tunnel 1 at Coal Creek after an overnight run from Salt Lake City in April 1962. Opposite, Colorado & Southern narrow gauge 65 is on the Leadville freight ready to leave Denver. September 1936. *Ray Hilner.* Two stations serve Colorado Springs, the Rio Grande on the west side of town for southbound trains and the Santa Fe along Pike's Peak Ave. on the east side — where Santa Fe Northern 3762 is about to depart for Denver in 1949. *Ross Grenard.*

Still seeing an occasional freight in the summer of 1
Chama, New Mexico comes to life as Denver & Rio Gra
483 and 498 prepare to attack the grades of Cumbres,
continue down to the security of the roundhouse in Alam
— not to venture out after the first heavy snow of win
In the last years before abandonment of many of the nar
gauge lines, the 268 makes an eastbound trip along
Gunnison River near Sapinero, Colorado in October 1
Robert W. Richardson. Northbound in the San Luis Va
near Alamosa is the 488 running through Estrella, Color
opposite. *Jim Shaughnessy.*

Just east of Thistle, Utah, Rio Grande 3711 works upgrade to gain some 2400 feet in elevation upon reaching Soldier Summit, less than 30 miles ahead. September 8, 1946. *John Maxwell.*

hen overland stages followed trails up and down mountain
ldernesses, a day's journey lay between points that are
w passed in an hour's ride. Then each peculiarity of na-
re was relatively more prominent than now and the name
was given usually had some local significance. Hence
hnson's Canyon, near Williams, Arizona, bearing the name
a one-time local character, is the setting for Santa Fe
mpound 2-10-2 1672 drifting across the trestle in 1910.
rther West, on the Arizona-California border, the Red
ck Bridge over the Colorado River at Topock, built for
Atlantic & Pacific RR., became part of U.S. 66 with the
ening of the present double track bridge in 1945.

In 1956, opposite, a Tracy-bound Southern Pacific freight gets underway on a rainy night from Oakland, Calif. with handsome streamlined 4-6-2 2484 on the point. In the distance, a cab-in-front and a switcher move through the yard tracks. *Richard Steinheimer.* The Scenic Limited, operated by the Missouri Pacific, Rio Grande and Western Pacific between St. Louis and San Francisco, heads west near Niles, Calif. behind 4-8-2 172, purchased by the Western Pacific from the Florida East Coast. *Fred Stoes.* The Milwaukee Road's Columbian crosses the Northern Pacific on its westward journey out of Spokane, Wash. in March 1951, right. *Philip R. Hastings.*

Arriving at Hillyard Yard in Spokane is Spokane, Portla[n]
& Seattle 911, a 4-6-6-4 of identical design and appearan[ce]
as those of the Great Northern and Northern Pacific, [on]
an eastbound extra. March 10, 1951. Below, at busy Ma[r]
shall, Wash., a favorite for photographer Hastings, Northe[rn]
Pacific 4-6-6-4 5116 with 5112 cut in ten cars back work[s]
an eastbound freight. Sept. 1950. Two photos, *Philip [J.]
Hastings.*

In a magnificent display of Union Pacific motive power, 3561 and 3821 doublehead an eastbound extra at Quartz, Oregon, in the shadow of the Blue Mountains. September 21, 1948. *Henry R. Griffiths.*

Into the Woods

the mid-1960's Rayonier Lumber still
ted steam power up into the dense
ts from Railroad Camp to Camp 3 on
ower end of the Olympic Peninsula in
tate of Washington. The two photos
depict one of their 2-6-6-2 tank loco-
ves, the 111, pulling empty log cars
f Railroad Camp and at the Camp 3
d, where the logs are transferred to
railroad from trucks hauling them
from higher elevations where they
cut. At one time a network of rail
penetrated deep into the mountains,
to be abandoned as the areas were
bed of timber, now being restored by
nier's extensive tree farm operations.

Below, Rayonier 111 pulls slowly into Railroad Camp from off of the Camp 3 branch with 23 loads in the usual rainy conditions to be found on the Peninsula. The 111 is a side tank locomotive, obtained from Weyerhaeuser along with the 110, and has been modified by the addition of an old Northern Pacific slope back tender. June 6, 1961. *John E. Shaw*. September of 1965 finds the 111 still active as it brings still another train of logs down from the reload, opposite. Rayonier 38, by way of the Weyerhaeuser and the Sierra Railroad, being too heavy for the Camp 3 line was used in the final years on the main line to the log dump at New London, north of Hoquiam, Washington. It was photographed at Railroad Camp in February 1964, opposite below.

The shops of the Rayonier at Railroad Camp were completely equipped for repairs and servicing of its steam motive power, even in 1964, below. On the left the 110 does some switching beside the water tank, supported by heavy timber. The morning of February 3, 1964 saw the 111 take water from Railroad Camp's leaky tank, then move out into the yard to pick up empties for Camp 3, opposite.

A Ten-Wheeler from the Union Pacific is at Railroad Camp of the Polson Logging Co. in April 1939, before that company was purchased by the Rayonier, above opposite. *Emery Roberts.* Class 1 roads engaged in logging operations in the Northwest include the Northern Pacific, with a log train led by 4-6-0 1372 on the Snoqualmie Branch out of North Bend, Washington in August 1955, opposite, and the Idaho Northern Branch of the Union Pacific with 2-8-0 529 on Train 385, listed in the Official Guide as a mixed train, near Smith's Ferry, Idaho, above. July 28, 1946. *Henry R. Griffiths.* The southern end of Vancouver Island, British Columbia, had steam power in logging service in recent years, right and on the next page. Here, MacMillan & Bloedel's 2-6-2 1077 is hitting the grade near Mile 7 on return half of the 32 mile round trip made twice daily between Nanaimo River reload camp and the Esquimalt & Nanaimo Railway Interchange. April 1964. *Dave Wilkie.*

Left, 2-8-2 16 of the Comox Logging & Railway brings a train of empty log cars up to the re-load from Ladysmith in May 1959. *John E. Shaw*. The 16, like most logging locomotives, has the usual cables and chains on the pilot in order to better cope with the unexpected. Canadian National Extra 2149 West is crossing the 614 foot Koksilah River trestle at Mile 51.1 on the Cowichan sub-division on September 16, 1958, below. *Dave Wilkie*.

With less than a month's service remaining, Klickitat Shay 7 heads north out of Klickitat, Washington for the reload. March 12, 1964. The eighteen miles of line have been abandoned, with trucks now being used to bring the logs down to the mill.

A wet spring snow is falling as Klickitat 7 leaves the re-load with its train of logs. Unloading operations are carried out at Klickitat, an interchange with the Spokane, Portland & Seattle Goldendale Branch north from the Columbia River, as the car sides are dropped, allowing the logs to roll into the mill pond, opposite. March 11, 1964. Here, the Washington, Idaho & Montana Railway, a common carrier from Palouse, Washington to Bovill, Idaho and with stations such as Princeton, Harvard, Yale, Stanford, Vassar and Cornell between these points, has a log train ready to leave the eastern terminus of the line. It is again seen near Bovill behind 2-8-0 21, below. Two photos, *Philip R. Hastings.*

Clover Valley Lumber 8, a 2-6-2 purchas[ed] from the Hobart Southern, brings a str[ing] of empty log cars up to Camp 14 on M[ay] 28, 1956, spring grass almost hiding [the] rails, left. The daily run to the woods [of] the Clover Valley's train here north of [the] Western Pacific main line crossing at Ha[w]ley, California in the spring was a sight [to] delight all lovers of steam railroading, [as] the meadows were carpeted with wildflo[w]ers and the sound of the whistle ech[oed] down the canyons. Opposite, the 4, a 2-6-[6] tank locomotive, works a carload of ti[es,] a crane, and 29 empties up a 4 perce[nt] grade to the lumber camp. May 28, 19[56.] The Clover Valley was sold to the Feath[er] River Lumber before the 1957 season a[nd] operations ceased later in that same ye[ar.] Three photos, *John E. Shaw*.

Narrow Gauge Shay 10 of the West Side Lumber approaches Tuolumne, California with a log train in 1957, above. *Philip R. Hastings.* Opposite, the West Side, located to the west of Yosemite National Park, has Shay 8 underway with a train of log headed for the mill at Tuolumne on June 1, 1956. *John E. Shaw.*

On the page opposite, West Side Shays 8 and 10 are once again heading for the mill at Tuolumne; this time in 1960, after the line had been purchased for the second time in its sixty year history by the Pickering Lumber, with the name remaining the same. With the passing of the West Side in 1961, it joined countless other logging roads, once covering the heavily forested mountains of the Far West, being abandoned only as the timber supply was exhausted or a more economical means of hauling logs was developed. Above, Pickering Shay 11 switches log cars into the mill at Standard, California in 1960. Three photos, *Gary Allen*.

At the western end of Western Pacific's scenic Feather River Canyon, the Feather River Railway heads east from this main line to Feather Falls, California. Above opposite, the number 3 is north of Bidwell Bar in June 1963, at a sight to be flooded by the reservoir backed up by the Oroville Dam. *Gary Allen.* Left, in the wet bottomlands of east Texas forests, 2-8-2 16 of Frost Lumber Industries Nacogdoches & Southeastern Railroad switches the mill at Nacogdoches in December 1946. *Robert W. Richardson.* Above, south of Flagstaff, Arizona, Southwest Lumber Mills 2-8-0 2 works her daily seven car train up the line from Allen Lake. February 22, 1957. *John E. Shaw.*

Southwest Lumber 2 was hauling logs to the mill pond at Flagstaff in August 1965, above opposite. *Gary Allen.* After a day's work, above, number 2 basks in the setting sun outside the engine house in Flagstaff. *John E. Shaw.* On the left in a May 1953 scene, Southwest Lumber 4, a 2-6-6-2, heads north for the mill. *Fred Ragsdale.*

At one time or another, most Western rail lines are faced with steep grades, must cross high mountain passes, or negotiate tight curves as they make their way across the Continent. In the two photos on this page, a heavy Colorado & Southern ore train makes a run for the grade that lies ahead as it pounds past the depot at Horse Creek, Wyo. behind 2-10-2 902. A few miles further south, the train has slowed to a little more than a walk as it nears the top of the grade. December 1, 1956. From below the cliffs where Indians once explored the upper reaches of the Yuba River, the City of San Francisco comes into sight with a one-unit booster ahead of its Alco PA-3's as it drops down toward Sacramento from Donner Summit on Southern Pacific's Overland Route near Crystal Lake, Calif. July 1966. *Richard Steinheimer.*

Crossing the Divide

Sixty-seven miles west of Reno in lonely Yuba Pass, Southern Pacific Train No. 27, the San Francisco Overland, drifts westward on February 3, 1956. Though in its declining years this train of such historic name still retained much of the romantic atmosphere and appointments so cherished by knowledgeable travelers of the pre-jet era. It was near this spot that the City of San Francisco was snowbound in January 1952. *Guy L. Dunscomb.* Between Lathrop and Niles, Calif., the Western Pacific climbs several hundred feet to reach Altamont Pass, left; where the Feather River Express, behind Ten-wheeler 78, crosses U.S. 50 and the Southern Pacific westbound near the top of the pass in 1937. Above, The Exposition Flyer with 4-8-2 179, is descending the pass near Livermore, Calif. in 1941. Two photos, *Fred C. Stoes.*

eneath weathered cliffs in historic Echo Canyon, Utah, Union Pacific 3709 helps at the rear of X1402 east on the steady rade out of Ogden, opposite. August 31, 1955. *Henry R. Griffiths*. Running southeast from Salt Lake City, the Rio Grande rosses the Wasatch Range at Soldier Summit. Above, leading an eastbound freight toward the summit, is 2-10-2 1403 with the 508, a 2-8-8-2, cut in the middle of the train as it passed Gilluly, Utah. June 30, 1941. Two photos, *John Maxwell*.

Early on an August morning in 1958, dur[ing]
a brief return of steam power acr[oss]
Wyoming's lonely, beautifully desol[ate]
Sherman Hill, Union Pacific Big Boy 4[019]
left Cheyenne in the chill of a late summ[er]
dawn. Having turned westward on the n[ew]
line at Speer, it heads into a deep cut n[ear]
Emkay, left. After a stop at Harriman [for]
coal and water, the 4019 slows for a st[op]
on the fill at Dale, which replaced the D[ale]
Creek trestles when the line was reloca[ted]
in the early 1900's. The two lines join [at]
this point only to separate again west [of]
Hermosa Tunnel. The City of Los Ange[les]
has passed as the 4019 again gets underw[ay]
amid thundering exhaust and the spray [of]
steam, opposite. August 24, 1958.

ILL

In 1957, *Philip Hastings* rode with Big Boy 4008 over the new line, opposite, nine miles longer between Cheyenne and Laramie but with more favorable grades than the line to the north, still used by passenger trains and eastbound freights. Above, the 4013 has just left the old line at Corlett Junction rolling west at sunrise. With 2-10-2 5317 as helper, extra 3953 attacks the Hill near Otto, Wyoming in November 1948, right.

Cresting the summit at Sherman in 1947 is eastbound extra 3959 at an elevation of 8013 feet, some 230 less than the town o[f] Sherman on the original main line, pushing westward during the spring of 1868. Rail Photo Service; *B. F. Cutler*. The statio[n] and other structures have vanished, leaving little trace of this famous landmark. Until several years ago, steam helpers fro[m] both Cheyenne and Laramie were turned here, running light downhill to their point of origin. Below, 4-6-6-4 3800 is on a wor[k] train near Buford, an important point in the early days of the railroad. *Don Ahlbeck*. On the page opposite, helper 5077, comin[g] down off the Hill, passes the tower at Borie. At one time this tower saw all main line traffic as well as trains up from Den[-]ver over the Borie Cut-off. Helper service continued through the summer of 1953, well after the opening of the new line, whic[h] was to immediately eliminate this necessity. Westbound at Borie in 1945 are 2-8-8-2's from the N&W and C&O, making slo[w] but steady progress with heavy war-time tonnage. Two photos, *Charles W. Burns*.

In the two views on this page, Union Pacific 4-12-2 9044 and 4-6-6-4 3989, below, are seen near Sherman when steam was still in command of the Hill. Opposite, with Mike 2294 helping, an eastbound freight approaches the west portal of Hermosa Tunnel where the diesel powered freight, its units 855 and 731 being followed by Burlington and Pennsylvania units, has just passed through. July 9, 1967.

The giant fill across Dale Creek at present-day Dale was a courageous undertaking for men and equipment in 1900. Completed in 1901, it replaced the precarious high trestle on the original main line which had crossed the creek some two miles upstream. The granite abutments for this trestle can still be seen above Dale Creek, as in the view from the west approach, right. A water tank was located between the cut, below, and the west end of the trestle. Above, opposite and on this page, Big Boy 4015 brings a westbound train over the new line at Dale and 4-8-4 835 has a train of Mail & Express eastbound on the fill, both in 1956. *Don Ahlbeck*. The City of Los Angeles approaches the old town-site of Dale Creek on an eastbound trip over Sherman in July 1967, opposite.

Two of the Santa Fe's principal grades between Chicago and Los Angeles are Raton Pass on the Colorado-New Mexico line and Cajon Pass in California, also used by the Union Pacific. Above, Cajon Pass in the days of steam, the roar of a brace of 2-10-2's on the rear of an eastbound freight near Alray is echoed by 2-8-2 3155 and the 3899 on the head end. October 5, 1947. *Walter Thrall,* John E. Shaw collection. Grades of the switchbacks over the top of the pass, used while the tunnel was being constructed, are visible above the train as 2-10-2 3913, assisted on the rear by 3898, approach Raton Tunnel with a westbound drag freight at Wootton, Colorado. April 14, 1953. Two photos, *Philip R. Hastings.*

The Colorado & Southern between Leadville and Climax, once part of the South Park Line over Kenosha and Boreas Pass, was still in steam in June 1961, opposite. *Gary Allen.* The north-south main line of the C&S is dominated by many grades, two of the most notable being into Palmer Lake, south of Denver, where 2-10-2 907 gets an assist from Ft. Worth & Denver Pacific 552 at Larkspur, Colo. in April 1952; and east of Boulder near Louisville with southbound freight 78 running several hours early on this day in May 1960.

As the rails were pushed westward, steep grades over high mountain passes were common to many of the lines. Add to this the heavy snows of winter and operating efficiency was greatly reduced, if not totally impossible. On the page opposite, the line of the Denver & Salt Lake over Rollins Pass, with an elevation of 11,680 at Corona, was in constant danger of snow slides throughout the many long winter months. The rotary plow and four locomotives were halted by one of these avalanches in the late spring of 1925 as they attempted to ascend the west side of the pass. One of the many mountain crossings made by the narrow gauge lines of the Denver & Rio Grande was over Poncha Pass, south of Salida, Colorado on the line through the San Luis Valley to Alamosa, where 2-8-2's 499 and 496 are fighting their way through drifts. January 28, 1949. *Robert W. Richardson*. Rotary plow 42, right, is on the Northern Pacific over Stampede Pass at Lester, Washington, high in the Cascades. January 1949. *Albert Farrow*. The Uintah, with some seventy miles of track from Mack, on the Denver & Rio Grande main line in extreme western Colorado, north to Watson, Utah, encountered 7.5 percent grades over Baxter Pass, where a wedge plow is at work clearing the line, below.

In the photo at the left, the descent of Baxter Pass is made by one of the two tank engines of the Uintah, the 21, pulling a single combine on the daily round trip between Dragon and Mack. Near the end of operations for this narrow gauge road, 2-6-6-2 50 rounds one of the tight curves up Baxter Pass above Atchee with a mixed train, below. May 9, 1939. *Otto Perry.* On the page opposite, Union Pacific 4-12-2 9029 is running down grade near Archer, Wyoming where it will soon follow Lodgepole Creek into the Platte River Valley of western Nebraska. December 22, 1940. *John W. Maxwell.*

Although the narrow gauge line of the Denver & Rio Grande Western crosses the Continental Divide at an elevation of only 7730 feet, a few miles west of Chama, New Mexico, the real challenge is on the 4 percent grade up Cumbres Pass, geographically located to the north and east of Chama. The summit, 10015 feet, is reached after fourteen miles of some of the most scenic mountain railroading to be found anywhere. On the left, Mikado 493 is climbing the grade with a short train near Lobato in September 1965. The summer of 1967 found only a few trips made between Alamosa and Chama as operations were greatly reduced. Above, the 483, with an assist from the 498, is working upgrade with empty and bad order cars for Alamosa. In August 1961, opposite, the 486 and 483 are near Cresco, below Windy Point—often closed by drifts during the winter months.

aching the top of the pass, opposite
, the 493 has left its train down of
loop to the east of the summit and
turned on the wye. After taking
ter, it will proceed downhill to
ama for the rest of the load. Right,
second turn arrives, backlighted by
ate afternoon sun and framed in the
wshed which protects the turning
e. Resting on the bridge over the
mbres Pass road, the 498 waits its
n for the water column, left.

Conducter Frank Young has a fresh supply of drinking water pumped from the crystal clear well at Cumbres, at the crest of the San Juan Range, and the 492 has turned on the wye to return light to Chama, above. April 11, 1953. *Philip R. Hastings.* Opposite, the 487 has encountered drifts, leaving snow and ice packed around its running gear as another storm moves in to isolate Cumbres Pass from the rest of the line during the well-remembered long winter of 1948-49. *Robert W. Richardson.* Long after the narrow gauge rails of both the Rio Grande Southern and Denver & Rio Grande had vanished from Ridgway, the roundhouse, where engines once looked out over the Uncompahgre Range to the east, stood desolate and abandoned.

hen the rails were taken up over Marshall Pass ring the summer of 1955, the highest crossing of e Continental Divide by the Rio Grande went th them. Opposite, Mikado 489 leads the scrap ain over the 10,856 foot summit. *Robert W. Rich- dson.* In 1963, the station and water tank at Sar- nts stood only as reminders of the days when 4- gine freights started the ascent of the west side the pass. Two of the Northern Pacific's grades hich require extra motive power are Stampede ass in the Cascades of Washington and on Boze- an Pass west of Livingston, Montana. Above, a mpound road engine is assisted by 2-8-2 1671 on estbound tonnage near Lester, Washington. *War- n Wing collection.* Over on the Rocky Mountain ivision, 2-8-8-4 5003 is helping on the rear of a estbound freight working its way to the tunnel at e top of the pass. July 5, 1951. *Philip R. Hastings.*

Along an Open Track

The yearly circus train from the museum in Baraboo, Wisconsin to Milwaukee for the parade was handled in 1966 by Burlington 4960, shortly before it was retired. Running over the C&NW, opposite, the Rock River is crossed at Jefferson Junction—while two days earlier, on June 28, the 4960 heads north through rural Wisconsin near Evansville, complete with an auxiliary tender from the Colorado & Southern and a C&NW bay-window caboose, right.

In 1967, the 5629, a Pacific originally owned by the Grand Trunk Western, was assigned to the circus train, shown at left approaching Devil's Lake, Wisconsin. Below, the Cole Bros. Circus came to Janesville, Wisconsin in 1947 and proceeded to unload wagons and equipment by means of two-horse teams as curious nonlookers watched the operation. Two photos, *Jim Walter*. Still operating steam power into the early 1960's was the 11 mile Duluth & Northeastern between Cloquet and Saginaw, Minnesota. Shown opposite is ex-Army 0-6-0 29 switching the Great Northern connection to a paper mill at Cloquet in 1962 and 2-8-0 16 making up its train at Saginaw for the downgrade trip to the mill. Two photos, *Philip R. Hastings* and *Jim Shaughnessy*.

For Railroad Costomers Only
Public Restrooms At Bath House
One Block East

With passenger service between Madison and Chicago now provided only by the Milwaukee Road, the *Sioux,* morning train to Chicago, gets out of Janesville, Wisconsin in the winter of 1965. Before the Chicago & North Western abandoned the six miles of track from Lake Geneva to Williams Bay, Wisconsin, railroad patrons had special privileges over those who made their way to this resort town by other means of transportation, opposite below. Two photos, *Jim Walter.* Above, C&NW 2-8-2 2600 is westbound on the Belt Line at Des Plaines, Illinois with a local freight. August 1948. *Fred C. Stoes.*

ne of the most frequently photographed "steam in the
0's" operations across the midwest were the numerous
xcursions of the Burlington behind 4-8-4's such as the
32 near Mendota, Illinois in March 1963, opposite.
im Walter. Train 190, the *Zephyr Rocket*, operated by
e Rock Island and Burlington between the Twin
ities and St. Louis, pauses in Waterloo, Iowa a few
*eeks before it was discontinued in April 1967. Right,
e Decorah Branch of the Rock Island in northern
wa saw its last train in November 1963 as Conductor
. C. Wright climbs aboard for the last time. Two pho-
s, *Philip R. Hastings*. Union Pacific mixed train 83,
elow, is running along the North Loup River near
otesfield, Nebraska behind 2-8-0 428 in its last year of
ervice. October 25, 1958. *J. W. Lozier*.

Mining, the sole purpose in building many an early day railroad, still requires many miles of track in a few widely spread areas of the mid-west and west. The Bevier & Southern, running ten miles south from the Burlington connection at Bevier, Missouri, has leased Burlington 4943 working the coal mine in 1961, right. *Philip R. Hastings.* Below, the copper hauling Magma Arizona with 2-8-0 5 on the point, heads a load downgrade near Queen for the Southern Pacific interchange at Magma. September 1961. The limestone quarry along Laramie River in Wyoming is operated by the Portland Cement Co., using an ex-UP 0-6-0 on a somewhat less than first class stretch of track across the plains, opposite. June 1961. *Gary Allen.*

The local freight on the Union Pacific's Boulder Branch, which saw its last steam power due to a 24 inch snow in April 1957, crosses the Colorado & Southern at Ara and heads east toward Erie, Colorado after a much lighter snowfall in February 1959, below. Against the front range of the Rockies, the water column on the Colorado & Southern stands as a memento of the past at Ara, Colorado, east of Boulder. *Don Ahlbeck*. Having left Denver at dawn, Union Pacific Big Boy 4007 is near Lucerne, Colorado bound for Laramie in December 1955.

Heading for the Portland Cement Co. plant, ex-UP switcher with a tender from a Consolidation pushes its loads across the Laramie River west of Laramie, Wyoming, opposite. August 31, 1962. The Great Western's home base of Loveland, Colorado provides the winter scenes here as 2-8-0 75 switches in the yard on a quiet Sunday afternoon in November 1958. On a considerably colder day in December 1961, a tank engine is switching cars of sugar beets, below.

East of Loveland, the Great Western crosses the Union Pacific branch to Ft. Collins and Buckeye at Kelim, where much-photographed Decapod 90 is enroute to Eaton, above opposite, in November 1960. Continuing on its journey, the 90 works upgrade, above, out of Officer Junction before descending Oklahoma Hill to Windsor, Colorado, left. December 13, 1961.

x miles east of Loveland, at Officer Junction, the other
in line of the Great Western turns south for Johnstown
d Longmont. Once again following the 90, opposite, it
rks upgrade south of Johnstown, ending its run in the
rds at Longmont, right. Completing this particular day's
ivity, the 90 picks up cars from the Union Pacific inter-
ange at Milliken, where at one time Great Western track-
e extended south to Wattenberg.

Catching up with the 90 at Windsor, above, tickets were purchased for a round trip ride in the caboose between Severance and Eaton. Welcome was the warmth of the caboose as we climbed aboard amid sub-zero temperatures of a Colorado winter on the plains. Stops were made enroute to pick up sugar beets that had fallen along the right-of-way, left, and to set out a few cars on the siding to be loaded with beets. The return trip into the sunset behind the 90 held memories of the steam era, soon to pass.

A Rio Grande stock extra, once an important part of its freight traffic, loads sheep at Jack's Cabin, Colorado on the Crested Butte Branch out of Gunnison while the locomotive, 2-8-0 278, takes water. September 20, 1952. *Philip R. Hastings*. At this time narrow gauge rails ran over one other branch line from Gunnison, fifteen miles to Castleton on the Baldwin Branch; as well as from Ridgway, still served by the standard gauge to Ouray, closely surrounded by rugged mountains. *Bob Richardson* photographed a caboose hop with 2-8-0 318 at Ouray in March 1953, opposite. The Silverton Branch north from Durango, Colorado continues to attract tourists with spectacular views such as the Canyon of the Animas River. *Dave Wilkie*.

From Louisiana's Tremont & Gulf Railway came Magma Arizona Mikado 7, posing for a handsome portrait at Superior, Arizona, left. *John E. Shaw*. Tombstone, Arizona, one of the last frontier towns of the west, is now just another ghost town without rail service. Back in April 1950 Southern Pacific mixed train 940 is arriving in Tombstone after a nine mile run from Fairbank behind 2-6-0 1624. *Fred Ragsdale*. San Diego & Arizona Eastern Railway trainmen pass their time at Dos Cabezas, California, in the Imperial Valley region, waiting for a meet with opposing train 452 from San Diego. Number 2700, a 2-8-0, will help on the point to the top of the hill at Hipass, where the Baldwin diesel will take the train on to San Diego. 1952. *Richard Steinheimer*.

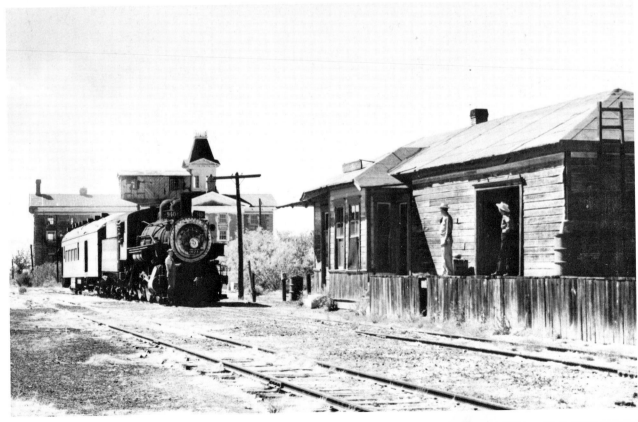

wo shortlines along the coast of southern
alifornia are the Ventura County Railway
d the Santa Maria Valley, shown below and
a the page opposite. Ventura County 2-6-2 2
near Oxnard, California with a two-car spe-
al in July 1960. *Gary Allen.* Opposite, 2-8-2 21
the Santa Maria Valley whistles for a road
ossing near Santa Maria on April 20, 1958.
uring the last regular steam operation on the
outhern Pacific narrow gauge, engineer Wal-
r Ferguson fills the tank at Kearsarge, in the
adow of Mount Whitney and a few miles
est of Death Valley, California, right. Two
otos, *John E. Shaw.*

On the page opposite, a Baldwin ten-wheeler built as Southern California 15 in 1887 and sold to the Santa Fe in 1898, works at Piedra, California in 1913, a year before being scrapped. The Sierra Railway, popular with fans and studios, teamed up 4-6-0 3 for Columbia Pictures "Iron Horse" TV series, shown at Jamestown, California in December 1965 and for a 1957 excursion near Keystone, California, above. Two photos, *Gary Allen* and *Philip R. Hastings.*

rough country once traversed by the row gauge Nevada-California-Oregon, thern Pacific Cab-Forward 4251 is near deline, in northern California, on August 31, 1955, left. Two *Fred Stoes* photophs, on this page and at the bottom of osite page, show double-headed Southᴘ Pacific Consolidations on the now ndoned Santa Cruz - Los Gatos line ough the California Redwoods. Oppo-, the 2781 and 2838 are north of Santa ız with a passenger extra in July 1938. th the 2838 again as the road engine, the 3 teams up as helper on a Convention cial at Rincon in 1937, right. Below, a l freight on the Santa Cruz Branch is dled by a pair of 2-8-0's in 1947. *Fred C.* es.

There has been no regularly scheduled passenger service on the Tillamook Branch of the Southern Pacific for well over thirty years, and it was over fifty years ago that the photograph at the top of the page opposite was made near Timber, Oregon. The Tillamook Branch extends westward from Hillsboro to Tillamook, some ninety-one miles constructed by the Pacific Railway & Navigation Co. and completed in 1911; but coming under control of the Southern Pacific in 1909. Under the operational set-up at the time, Train 141 ran over five branches: Milwaukie, Newberg, Tigard, West Side, and finally the Tillamook Branch. The lead engine is an 1892 Schenectady built 4-8-0, the second engine a 4-6-0. Timber, Oregon, in the winter of 1915, had 4-8-0 2931 equipped with plow, standing alongside the trim log depot, opposite bottom. Timber was one of the most important locations on the Tillamook Branch, for it was here that the Southern Pacific maintained a roundhouse that serviced the many locomotives used on the branch. At the right, Southern Pacific 2949 is at Timber in 1916. Below, at Timber during the summer of 1914, 4-8-0's 2932 and 2947, with the latters' tender lettered Central Pacific, await their assignments. Four photos, *H. H. Arey,* from Guy L. Dunscomb collection.

The lower photo on the opposite page shows still another view on the Tillamook Branch, with Southern Pacific 2928 near Wedeburg, Oregon, in 1914. Above, the Portland to Dallas, Oregon local passenger is at St. Joseph about 1909 behind 4-4-0 1509. St. Joseph was the junction of the West Side and Newberg Branches from Portland, both of which were electrified in 1912, with electrification being abandoned about 1929. Two photos, *H. H. Arey*, from Guy L. Dunscomb collection. Out on the deserts of Eastern Washington is the east end of the Milwaukee Road's Cascade electrification. Right, at Othello in March 1953, a roundhouse worker puts up the white flags on a 2-8-2 scheduled to head a branch line train, while in the distance one of the big GE units waits for a train to come in off the Idaho Division. *Richard Steinheimer.*

On the opposite page, Milwaukee 2-6-6-2 58 works north up the Pend Oreille River valley near Dalkena, in the northeast corner of Washington, with freight No. 291 for Metalline Falls in 1950. Left, Northern Pacific 2-8-0 25 is switching in the yard at Wallace, Idaho, on the branch line from Missoula, Montana over Lookout Pass. September 2, 1950. An October 1950 scene at Arrow, Idaho, below, finds Northern Pacific 2-8-2 1748 as rear helper on freight No. 662 running from Lewiston to Spokane, Washington. Three photos, *Philip R. Hastings.*

Across Endless Miles

The Milwaukee's "Yellowstone Park Line" branches off from the main at Three Forks, Montana and heads south to Gallatin Gateway. Opposite, the 1029, a 4-6-0, is assigned to the local freight getting underway a mile out of Three Forks. July 4, 1951. *Philip R. Hastings.* Above, Colorado & Southern 2-10-2 900 passes a water hole in the cattle grazing country of northern Colorado on its run from Denver to Cheyenne. October 4, 1958.

Under a blue Colorado sky, Colorado & Southern train No. 8 takes the siding at Winchell for a meet with train No. 1, the "Texas Zephyr" on April 14, 1953, above left. *Philip R. Hastings*. East of the summit of Cumbres Pass, the Rio Grande narrow gauge winds its way along the Los Pinos River, opposite below, before turning east for Osier, Toltec, Sublette and Big Horn as it descends the grade into Antonito, Colorado; once the junction point of the line to Santa Fe, New Mexico. An earlier narrow gauge line of the Rio Grande, now abandoned, was over Cerro Summit east of Montrose, Colorado, right, where 2-8-0 361 has a short westbound freight in tow in May 1949. *M. W. Swansick*. Heading out over the eastern plains of Colorado, Rock Island's "Rocky Mountain Rocket" has left Colorado Springs and Pike's Peak in the distance, below. At Limon, this section, powered by 4-6-2 900, will connect with the section from Denver before continuing its eastward journey. October 15, 1949.

nbing out of the Imperial Valley from
Centro, in extreme southern California,
San Diego & Arizona Eastern crosses
ely Carriso Gorge, where a track watch-
gazes down from the high trestle at
nel 15 in 1952, opposite above. *Richard*
inheimer. Having crossed the vast Mo-
Desert, an eastbound Santa Fe freight
ves in Needles, California at sunset
ind eight units. April 9, 1964. At the
t, an inspection car on Colorado's nar-
gauge Uintah Railway descends Bax-
Pass above Atchee. The Rio Grande
fornia Zephyr, below, is starting its
ab up the front range of the Rockies
t of Denver at Arena. May 1961.

ust before the end of steam operation on Mixed train 353 between Yoder and Cheyenne, 4-8-2 7862 is at work through some ugged Wyoming terrain north of Albin on February 19, 1956. *Neal Miller*. Left, Union Pacific 4-6-6-4 3833 pulls a westbound xtra along the Snake River west of King Hill, Idaho. May 23, 1948. *Henry R. Griffiths*. Nearing the top of the grade, Colorado Southern 2-10-2 900 is hard at work a few miles south of Horse Creek, Wyoming with a heavy train of ore. January 11, 1959.

In the Blue Mountains of eastern Oregon in the background, Union Pacific 4-6-6-4 3816 pulls 86 cars of eastbound tonnage through Hot Lake on September 12, 1957, left. *Henry R. Griffiths*. Not having operated regular passenger service since 1941, the Nevada Northern runs an occasional excursion using 4-6-0 40, below, shown here near McGill, Nevada on April 7, 1957. *John E. Shaw*. At the right, a boiler keeps steam up at the East Ely engine house for a 1964 trip. *Gary Allen*.

An Idaho shortline with some 13 miles of track between Nezperce and Craigmont is the Nezperce Railroad, opposite top, its motive power being 2-6-2 9, once owned by the Amador Central, McCloud River, and Yreka Western, shown with three cars of grain for the Camas Prairie Railroad at Craigmont. June 14, 1951. Left, silhouetted against a late afternoon sky, Milwaukee ten-wheeler 1029 is on the "Yellowstone Park Line" near Logan, Montana with a local freight. July 4, 1951. In western Montana, the main line of the Northern Pacific branches at Logan; one line going to Butte and the other to the capital city of Helena, where Extra 2607 west is at Toston, above. When Nezperce & Idaho 4-4-0 4 (ex Northern Pacific 684) was discovered rusting away in the weeds at Nezperce, Idaho, the Northern Pacific transported it to Spokane, Washington for reconditioning. Below, doubleheaded 2-8-2's 1781 and 1792 head a northbound gravel train which included the 1883 American Standard in its consist, as seen near Spangle, Washington on June 4, 1951. Four photos, *Philip R. Hastings.*

Through
the
Rockies

...st out of the tunnel at the summit of Bozeman Pass are five units of an ...stbound Northern Pacific freight, left, drifting down the almost 2 percent ...ade toward Livingston, Montana, fifteen miles ahead. September 23, 1964. ...ossing the Bitter Root Range between Mullan, Idaho and Saltese, Montana ...s no easy task even for the big Northern Pacific Z-3 Compounds. At the ...ht, ten cars are all that the 4020 can handle in arriving at the summit of ...okout Pass in February 1951. Below, the 4021 is starting up the rugged 4 ...rcent grade westbound from Saltese. September 2, 1950. Two photos, ...ilip R. Hastings.

A 1956 excursion on the Coalmont Branch of the Union Pacific, above, found 2-8-0 535 with seven cars on the grade above Albany, Wyoming. This line, now operating only as far south as Hebron, Colorado, is the only rail into the North Park area of Colorado, although other routes were contemplated. Below, shops and facilities of the Uintah Railway were nestled in a mountain valley at Atchee, Colorado, on the south side of Baxter Pass. On part of the original narrow gauge main line of the Denver & Rio Grande, running west from Salida over Marshall Pass, through the Black Canyon of the Gunnison and across Cerro Summit into Montrose, 2-8-2 456, opposite, is at Cimarron, Colorado in October 1945, four years before this trackage was removed. *Robert W. Richardson.*

Opposite top, the San Juan, last of many early Colorado narrow gauge passenger trains, works up the east approach to Cumbres Pass near Los Pinos on Christmas day in 1948. Below, Rio Grande 2-8-0 1177 crosses a snow-covered trestle on the Creede Branch west of Alamosa, Colorado. January 18, 1949. Two photos, *Robert W. Richardson*. Rio Grande Southern Galloping Goose 5 gets its radiator cooled at Leopard Creek, Colorado, above, in June 1945.

From high above Windy Point, left, Rio Grande narrow gauge 2-8-2 484, assisted by the 488, has passed Coxo, Colorado on its steady 4 percent assault of Cumbres Pass. July 23, 1963. Right, Rio Grande Southern 2-8-2 455 is a few miles out of Ridgway at Sams on its 160-mile trip to Durango on March 29, 1950. A month before the Rio Grande Southern ceased operation, 2-8-2 461 takes a short train over a trestle between Gallagher and Coke Oven's in the Lizard Head Pass area of south-western Colorado, below. November 17, 1951. *Robert W. Richardson.*

The route of the Denver & Salt Lake Railroad climbed out of the valley along South Boulder Creek, right, and crossed the Continental Divide over the mountains at the top of the photo at Corona. Here, on a 1965 excursion, ex Great Western 2-8-0 51 approaches Rollinsville, Colorado. Below, three levels of the beginning grade over the pass are clearly visible from a point a few miles to the east of the present Moffat Tunnel. Opposite, below, Denver & Salt Lake 2-8-0 122 is at East Portal with the morning train to Craig, Colorado in 1947. *Forrest Crossen.* Above, one of the first trains through the tunnel, opened February 26, 1928, emerges from the west portal at Winter Park, Colorado behind Denver & Salt Lake 2-6-6-0 200.

The narrow gauge Argentine Central, climbing from Silver Plume, Colorado to an elevation of 13,100 feet on the side of Mt. McClellan, served the Waldorf and Vidler mines near the summit of Argentine Pass. Above, looking south in a 1910 photo from the Waldorf Mine, the Vidler Mine and the road over the pass are in the distance. Below, a Colorado & Southern passenger train, pulled by 2-8-0 69, takes water in Clear Creek Canyon between Golden and Idaho Springs on Janury 30, 1939. *Ray Hilner.* In earlier days the Colorado & Southern ran through passenger cars over the sixteen miles of the Argentine Central to Mt. McClellan.

Over rails of the one-time narrow gauge Colorado & Southern and preceding companies—Denver, South Park & Pacific and Denver, Leadville & Gunnison—Colorado & Southern 2-8-0 641 proceeds cautiously downhill between Climax and Leadville, right, near the end of some 86 years of steam operation of this line. September 15, 1960. Behind a converted 0-6-0 purchased from the U.S. Army, Midland Terminal 2-6-0 64 starts up Ute Pass above Manitou Springs, Colorado bound for Cripple Creek, below. Here, in February 1949, the Midland Terminal has been given approval to cease operations and abandon the road, last segment of the old Colorado Midland from Colorado Springs to Divide, purchased by the Midland Terminal in 1921.

In the spring of 1951, a Rio Grande freight drag inches its way up Tennessee Pass behind a 4-unit diesel and a 3600 series 2-8-8-2 spotted in the middle of the train and the 3609 at the rear, opposite page and above, near Mitchell, Colorado. Three photos, *C. W. Burns*. Below, westbound train No. 1, the Scenic Limited, leaves Salida, Colorado behind Rio Grande 4-8-4 1803 in 1939. *Fred C. Stoes*.

Two compound locomotives of the Denver & Salt Lake, 2-6-6-0's 203 and 212, each with an extra water car, work a westbound freight across the Coal Creek Canyon Road west of Denver, above. From this point, they will start upgrade to tunnel 1, below, where Denver & Salt Lake ten-wheeler 303 was photographed with a mail car and coach for Craig, some 200 miles to the west. Two photos, *Forrest Crossen*. At the top of the opposite page, the predecessor of the Denver & Rio Grande California Zephyr, train No. 6, the Exposition Flyer, is eastbound out of Tunnel 3 north of Plainview, Colorado, behind 2-8-2 1203 on June 18, 1939. *Otto Perry.* Below, a Rio Grande freight is at Burns, Colorado, on the Dotsero Cutoff along the Colorado River. August 28, 1950. *John Maxwell.*

In the narrows of Glenwood Canyon, five units of the Denver & Rio Grande have an eastbound freight in tow beside the churning Colorado River below Shoshone, June 20, 1965.

To the Pacific

Northern Pacific Portland-Seattle pool train 407 passes Day Island as it approaches Tacoma, Washington along the blue waters of Puget Sound. June 22, 1963.

Close to the 9:45 p.m. departure time, Northern Pacific's Mainstreeter is ready to leave King Street Station in Seattle on the night of August 23, 1964, left. A rather unique operation of the Northern Pacific at Tacoma, Washington, below, was the backing of train 422 from Seattle out of Union Station to a higher grade level, from where it would proceed up grade to South Tacoma and over the Prairie, American Lake and Grays Harbor Line to Hoquiam. October 31, 1950. *Philip R. Hastings.*

Left, Northern Pacific 2-8-2 1800 is on the 15th Street bridge in Tacoma with the local freight to Mobase, a few miles south on the Prairie Line, in 1955. *J. M. Fredrickson*. Northern Pacific train 408, having left Union Station, tunnels under Ruston at the northern tip of Tacoma near Point Defiance Park, below, then travels along Puget Sound on its three hour trip to Portland. August 22, 1964.

the page opposite, top, North-
Pacific 4-8-4 2610 hustles a
ttle Time Special south
ough Steilacoom, Washington
a foggy day in December 1954.
M. Fredrickson. Below, North-
Pacific 2-8-2's 1708 and 1802
k their train to the yard after
ning into Tacoma from Port-
d over the Prairie Line. Octo-
31, 1950. *Philip R. Hastings.*
ling across Montana at 65 mph,
engineer of Great Northern's
pire Builder, aboard 4-8-4 2587,
iews his train orders, right.
l Photo Service, *B. F. Cutler.*
low, Union Pacific 2-8-8-0 3553
97 cars eastbound up the heavy
ade of Baker, Oregon. May 18,
7. *Henry R. Griffiths.*

Westbound in Oregon's Burnt River Canyon, Union Pacific X871 with five GP-30's is near Durkee with 100 cars on March 15, 1964, left. *Henry R. Griffiths.* Northern Pacific Mikes 1781 and 1792 are ready to leave Marchall, Washington, right, after bringing Nezperce & Idaho 4-4-0 4 in from the Idaho shortline at Nezperce. June 4, 1951. Climbing out of the Spokane River valley after leaving Spokane, Washington, Spokane, Portland & Seattle 4-6-6-4 900 parallels the Northern Pacific and Union Pacific main lines at Marchall, below. April 21, 1951. Two photos, *Philip R. Hastings.*

Outlined in smoke and steam, Spokane, Portland & Seattle 4-6-6-4 900 bursts from Tunnel 19 on the 1 percent grade westbound out of the Spokane River valley in 1950, left. Below, SP&S 4-8-4 700 wheels a freight across the Great Northern trestle over the Spokane River, May 15, 1951. Opposite, a Milwaukee Road freight, behind 4-6-2 889, has trackage rights over the Union Pacific trestle westbound from Spokane. January 28, 1951. Three photos, *Philip R. Hastings.*

STATION
ONE MILE

105
3

67

Union Pacific train 67 leaves Spokane on its daytime roundtrip to Wallace, Idaho, opposite, behind Pacific 3223. *Philip R. Hastings.* Right, Union Pacific 2-8-2 2209 is on the Milwaukee electrified line with a local freight at Sumner, Washington. February 28, 1948. *Albert Farrow.* Below, Great Northern 2-8-8-2 2042 passes the Ballard Station in Seattle as it begins an eastbound trip across the Cascade Mountains and through the almost 8-mile long Cascade Tunnel.

Canadian National train 587, below, headed by 2-8-0 2128 climbs heavy grade at Tidewater sub-division between Tyup and Deerholm, B.C. with empties for Youbou mill at Cowihan Lake on Vancouver Island. January 1957. *Dave Wilkie.*

Left, Canadian Pacific motor 9054 crosses trestle at milepost 14.6 on the normally "freight only" Port Alberni sub-division of the Esquimalt & Nanaimo with a westbound passenger extra above Cameron Lake. October 6, 1963. Canadian National 2-8-0 2149, below, switches loads of lumber on the dock at Cowichan Bay, B.C., terminus of the Tidewater sub-division on Vancouver Island. October 1958. Two photos, *Dave Wilkie.*

Between excursion assignments, Union Pacific 4-8-4 8444 roamed over parts of the system that had not seen steam power for many years. Above, it assists two diesel units with an extra freight west of The Dalles, Oregon, along the Columbia River. August 8, 1966. *Gary Allen.* Left, Southern Pacific Cab-forward 4204 backs from the wye tunnel at Cascade Summit, Oregon. Rail Photo Service, *B. F. Cutler.* Heading east for Donner Pass, the City of San Francisco is above Colfax, California on the Southern Pacific's line through the Sierras, opposite. May 1967. *Richard Steinheimer.*

In the opinion of many devoted railroad historians, the period between the two World Wars was the greatest era in American railroading—an era remembered and its passing lamented by many. Above is the Southern Pacific station at Sacramento, California about 1920. Inside can be seen the observation car of the train El Dorado, one of the many Sacramento Locals; to the left locomotive 1737, a Baldwin-built 2-6-0 of 1901 vintage that later spent many years on the Southern Pacific of Mexico, and to the right engine 2260, a trim little Class T-1 4-6-0 built by Schenectady in 1896. While part of this old structure, built by the Central Pacific in the 1870's, still stands, its use for passenger trains was supplanted in 1926 with the completion of a handsome brick station located just a couple of hundred yards to the rear and left of this pleasant scene. *D. L. Joslyn,* collection of G. L. Dunscomb.

Above, the West Coast Limited of the Southern Pacific is southbound in the Sacramento River Canyon below Dunsmuir, California in 1937. *Fred C. Stoes.* Southern Pacific commuter train 113 gets underway northbound out of San Jose for San Francisco at 5:06 a.m. on an August morning in 1956 behind 4-8-4 4446, right. *John E. Shaw.*

Southern Pacific Mail & Express train 72, opposite above, is southbound at Logan, California—pulled by the fore-runner of the "Daylight" locomotive, 4-8-2 4356. Left, Southern Pacific 2301, a Ten-wheeler, handles a train of empties for the rock quarry at Logan, east of Watsonville Jct., California. The Morning Daylight, above, is running at high speed near Aromas, California, southbound from San Francisco to Los Angeles behind 4-8-4 4458 in 1941. Three photos, *Fred C. Stoes.*

At the left, Southern Pacific 2-10-2 3744 is working an eastbound freight south of Watsonville Jct., California. *Fred C. Stoes.* Below, on November 23, 1947, the San Joaquin Daylight was powered by 4-8-2's 4352 and 4353, shown rounding a curve west of Saugus, California. In a similar view, Southern Pacific cab-forward 4213, opposite, heads the 51-car Mojave Local west of Saugus on August 14, 1949. Two photos, *Walter Thrall,* J. E. Shaw collection.

Electric Lines

Two days before scheduled operations of service ended on the Chicago, North Shore & Milwaukee, car 413 is ready to leave Mundelein, Illinois eastbound for Chicago, opposite. January 19, 1963. *Robert P. Olmsted.* The yard of the Illinois Central suburban electrics is filled at midmorning after the daily commuter rush into Chicago, above, has ended. Car 102 of the Chicago, South Shore & South Bend, right, stands beneath the Prudential Building in Chicago. February 1966.

South Shore 111, left, climbs the eastbound grade onto elevated trackage after leaving the Hammond, Indiana station. January 28, 1964. On a cold night in March 1964, below, South Shore 803 is on an eastbound freight in Burnham Yard, Chicago, ready to depart for Michigan City, Indiana; where the road's shops and yards are located, opposite. Three photos, *Robert P. Olmsted.*

Above, North Shore 764 pauses at the Lake Bluff, Illinois station at the head of a southbound train. January 11, 1963. *Robert P. Olmsted.* A work unit of the Milwaukee Electric Railway & Light Co. stands neglected and in need of repair, left, at East Troy, Wisconsin in July 1966. A single unit on the Fort Dodge, Des Moines & Southern, opposite top, crosses a high trestle over the Des Moines River west of Boone, Iowa. *Basil W. Koob.* Carrying and displaying their own advertising, car 72 of the Union Electric Railway is near Parsons, Kansas on February 3, 1946. *Ray Hilner.*

The Milwaukee Road's Olympian of the late 1920's, behind unit 10100, is descending the eastern slope of the Rockies near Piedmont, Montana, opposite top. Left, Milwaukee Bi-polar electric E-2, at Tacoma, Washington, will pull the Olympian Hiawatha backward to Seattle where it will couple on the head end for its eastbound run to Othello, eastern end of the Coast Division electrification. November 1, 1950. *Philip R. Hastings.* Through a spring rainstorm in the Cascades of Washington state, Milwaukee E42A, the Cedar Falls helper, rolls light downgrade toward Cedar Falls over the Mine Creek trestle after helping time freight 264 to the top of the grade at Hyak, above. March 1967. *Richard Steinheimer.*

The end of passenger service on the Yakima Valley Transportation Company is near in this 1947 view of car 7 in Yakima, Washington, opposite top. The last remnant of passenger equipment on the Butte, Anaconda & Pacific, a combination coach-baggage car, is behind unit 64 on a work train at Anaconda, Montana in August 1961, left. Winding deep into the bottom of the open pit copper mine at Bingham Canyon, Utah, unit 755 of the Kennecott Copper Corporation returns with empties for another load, above. September 1965.

Running over the old Bingham & Garfield, 2 units of the 16 mile Kennecott Copper electric line from Bingham Canyon to the smelter at Garfield, at the southern end of Great Salt Lake, handle some 60 cars of ore, left. September 1965. Below, car 825 of the Denver Tramways turns on the loop at Union Station on August 21, 1946. *Ray Hilner.*

On one of several trips operated by the Rocky Mountain Railroad Club over the Denver & Intermountain, car 25 is near Golden, Colorado, right. Cable car 504 of the San Francisco Muncipal Railway is stopped near the turntable at Bay and Taylor Streets in June 1948, below. Metropolitan Transit Authority car 1519 is Los Angeles bound in the night photo of April , 1961. *John E. Shaw.*

INDEX OF PHOTOGRAPHS

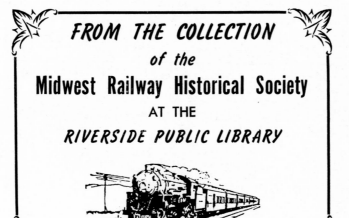